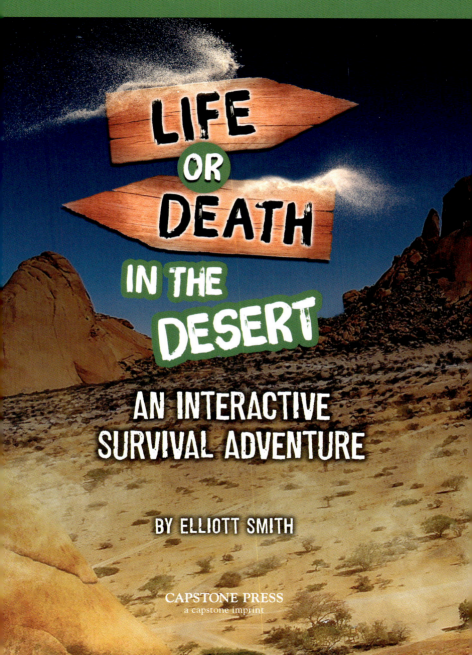

YOU CHOOSE

LIFE OR DEATH IN THE DESERT

AN INTERACTIVE SURVIVAL ADVENTURE

BY ELLIOTT SMITH

CAPSTONE PRESS
a capstone imprint

Published by Capstone Press, an imprint of Capstone
1710 Roe Crest Drive, North Mankato, Minnesota 56003
capstonepub.com

Copyright © 2025 by Capstone. All rights reserved. No part of this publication may be reproduced in whole or in part, or stored in a retrieval system, or transmitted in any form or by any means, electronic, mechanical, photocopying, recording, or otherwise, without written permission of the publisher.

Library of Congress Cataloging-in-Publication Data is available on the Library of Congress website.

ISBN: 9781669088431 (hardcover)
ISBN: 9781669088400 (paperback)
ISBN: 9781669088417 (ebook PDF)

Summary: Readers face the challenges of being lost in the desert, inspired by the experiences of real people.

Editorial Credits
Editor: Mandy Robbins; Designer: Dina Her; Media Researcher: Jo Miller; Production Specialist: Tori Abraham

Image Credits:
Getty Images: bonodo, 25, ROBERT DUNCAN/WEST AUSTRALIAN/AFP, 107, Ted Mead, 87, 93; Shutterstock: Andocs, 13, AzizAlbagshi, 49, b-hide the scene, 30, Benny Marty, 74, ChameleonsEye, 52, Dan Kosmayer, 78, Emily Marie Wilson, 62, fogcatcher, 4, 10, 102, freedom100m, 100, Ken Griffiths, 88, Peter Hermes Furian, 6, Ryan M. Bolton, 35, SCStock, 16, T. Schneide, cover, 1, VicVa, 71, Volodymyr Burdia, 42, Vova Shevchuk, 44; Wikimedia: History of Mercer County, Ohio, and Representative Citizens, Volume 1, 1907, 106

Design Elements:
Shutterstock: fogcatcher, Here, Mariyana M, oxinoxi, piyaphong, Vandathai, VRVIRUS

Any additional websites and resources referenced in this book are not maintained, authorized, or sponsored by Capstone. All product and company names are trademarks™ or registered® trademarks of their respective holders.

Printed and bound in the USA. 6121

TABLE OF CONTENTS

INTRODUCTION
ABOUT YOUR ADVENTURE 5

CHAPTER 1
A DESERT TREK......................7

CHAPTER 2
AFRICAN ADVENTURE................. 11

CHAPTER 3
HEADING TO ASIA 45

CHAPTER 4
QUEST DOWN UNDER.................75

CHAPTER 5
BE PREPARED......................101

    TRUE STORIES OF SURVIVAL..... 106
    S.T.O.P. TO SURVIVE 108
    OTHER PATHS TO EXPLORE 109
    GLOSSARY..................... 110
    READ MORE 111
    INTERNET SITES 111
    ABOUT THE AUTHOR 112

INTRODUCTION
ABOUT YOUR ADVENTURE

YOU are lost in the desert. Being alone in this isolated location will test your survival skills to the fullest. Fear and danger are your constant companions. Threats are everywhere—hunger, thirst, scorching heat, and predators. It's a constant struggle just to live through another day. YOU CHOOSE what path to take. Will you survive this unforgiving terrain and find your way to safety?

Turn the page to begin your adventure.

CHAPTER 1
A DESERT TREK

You have always been interested in the outdoors, especially the vast spaces of the desert. You are one of the members of the Outdoor Exploration Club at your university. It's a small club that's just been selected for a BIG prize! Each member gets an all-expenses paid trip to investigate the desert of their choice. There are also additional chances for special adventures within each trip. It's a once-in-a-lifetime opportunity!

Turn the page.

But before you pack your gear, the group needs to decide on a destination. You've narrowed it down to three continents.

You could go on a breathtaking trek to Africa. You imagine walking alongside pyramids and spotting some of the world's most dangerous wildlife. You could travel to Asia and get an up close look at one of the biggest bodies of sand in the world. There you might experience the drastic temperature changes of a cold desert filled with twinkling stars and unique plant life.

Or you can travel to the rough and rugged lands of Australia. Spiders there are as huge as the rocks that line the desert territory. Some of Australia's barren deserts are even surrounded by snowcapped mountains!

No matter which you choose, your group's adventure promises to be filled with opportunities to see things you could have never imagined. Which desert journey will you select?

- To trek African deserts, turn to page 11.
- To help with research in Asian deserts, turn to page 45.
- To explore the Australian outback, turn to page 75.

CHAPTER 2
AFRICAN ADVENTURE

You've studied so many books about Africa, it's hard to imagine not going there now that you have the opportunity.

"I'm voting for Africa," you say.

"Me too!" says Professor Tremblay, the group sponsor.

Before you know it, it's time to leave. Your small group gathers at the airport to prepare for the long flight to Africa. Your backpack is filled with journals to document your journey.

Turn the page.

Just then, one of your friends taps you on the shoulder. "Check out my new camera," Maria says. "I can't wait to take pictures of all the animals we'll see."

"That looks amazing," you say. In return, you tell Maria about your multiuse tool that's packed safely in your checked luggage.

The flight to Africa is long. At first, you're so excited you can't stop bouncing. But eventually, you fall asleep. A sharp *BUMP!* wakes you up as the plane lands in Marrakesh, Morocco.

As everyone collects their baggage, Professor Tremblay gathers the group. "Listen up, everyone," she says. "We are splitting into two groups. You can take a bus for a tour of the Sahara Desert or another plane to go to the Central Kalahari Game Reserve in Botswana."

You are torn. The Sahara features some of the biggest sand dunes in the world! And the Kalahari is home to some of the coolest creatures on the planet. You watch as people scramble to pick their activity. What do you choose?

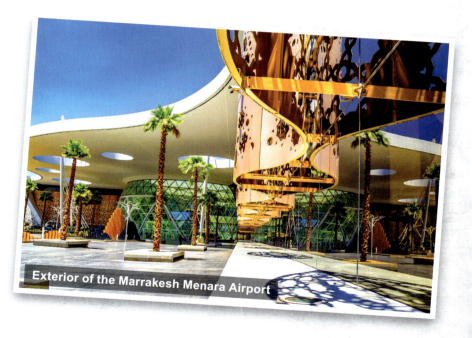
Exterior of the Marrakesh Menara Airport

- To head to the Sahara, turn to page 14.
- To check out the Kalahari, turn to page 23.

"I don't want to miss out on exploring the Sahara," you say to Professor Tremblay. "Did you know there are tons of fossils hidden there?"

"Well, I hope you find one," she says. "Let's head over to our bus."

The temperature is cooler than you expected as you step out of the airport. But it is morning after all.

The small group piles into the bus. The driver greets everyone with a wave.

The ride to camp will take several days, and you'll be stopping at various places on the way. As you leave Marrakesh, you're surprised at all of the greenery and large hills.

"We're in the foothills of the Atlas Mountains," Professor Tremblay explains.

After a couple hours, the bus stops at a café. The area is more modern and developed than the desolate desert you'd been envisioning, but the weather is definitely heating up.

After another hour and a half drive, you're high in the Atlas Mountains. There is less greenery, but this still isn't the flat desert you'd been expecting. The mountain views are gorgeous, though. The bus stops again in Ait-Ben-Haddou. The village of red clay homes looks like it's been carved right out of the hillside. The professor tells you that this village is around 400 years old.

"There's a camel!" someone shouts.

Sure enough, camels are being walked by locals alongside the road. You can hardly believe you are here!

Turn the page.

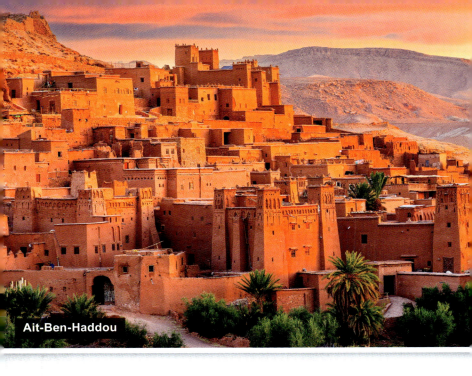

Ait-Ben-Haddou

You and your friend Tony spend the night in another village farther on and stay in a clay hotel room with a bamboo ceiling. You can hardly sleep for your excitement.

As you get on the desert road the next morning, the landscape is looking more like what you'd expected. The rocky, sandy landscape is dotted by brush and not much else.

The bus bumps along the desolate road. Every few hours, you're surprised by a town or village oasis in the barren, rocky landscape. Sometimes the bus stops, and sometimes it doesn't.

It's odd how the desert landscape can be broken up by these lush green, bustling villages. Many have shops and restaurants set up for tourists.

By late afternoon, you're finally in a dry stretch of flat, sandy desert.

That's more like it, you think.

As you look out the window, you notice that the sky is changing. The bright blue color is turning dark. The wind whips outside the bus.

"Sandstorm!" the driver yells.

Turn the page.

Like a sonic boom, a force suddenly hits the bus. Wind and sand swirl around the vehicle. You can hardly see anything through the angry cloud of sand. Some of your classmates are screaming. The bus rocks back and forth. It feels like the sandstorm will last forever. But suddenly, it stops. The sky turns blue again.

"Is everyone okay?" the driver asks. You all nod, dumbstruck. The driver turns the bus back on. But after about five minutes, the vehicle shudders to a stop. Steam seeps from the hood. The driver gets out to see what is wrong. Professor Tremblay joins him.

"Listen up," she says when she returns. "The bus is damaged from the sandstorm. So is the radio. We are still about 10 miles away from our next stop."

A murmur of worry circulates in the bus. *Are we stuck here?* you wonder.

You step off the bus to explore your surroundings. The heat is brutal. There is sand as far as the eye can see. There are some flat landscapes but also giant dunes that loom over the group.

"Some of us are going to try to get help," your friend Tony says. "And some people are going to stay with the bus and wait."

If you go for help, you'll get to civilization sooner, but sticking around the bus would give you the opportunity to do some exploration.

"What do you want to do?" Tony asks you.

- To walk through the desert, turn to page 20.
- To stay near the bus, turn to page 34.

"I'll go get help," you say. "I can't sit and wait."

A few others, including Tony, your friend Erin, and a guide named Sharif, join you in the hike toward camp. You all gather your supplies. You pull out your trusty compass and ask Sharif which direction the group should go.

"Let's head west," Sharif says. "There is a small village about five miles straight west, but it is seven miles by road."

The walk is slow and hot. No one wants to tire themselves out, so conversation is limited. You stay toward the back. Every so often, the wind kicks up a mini tornado of sand. You're glad you're wearing sunglasses.

Tony drops back to walk next to you. He's sweating profusely and is about to take off his shirt for relief.

"No!" you shout. "Keep yourself covered. Exposing more skin to the sun can lead to dehydration."

"Oh, right," he says, rolling down his sleeves. "How long do you think we have to go?"

"A few more miles," you say, squinting into the distance.

Before long, the sweat is pouring off your face. You're starting to feel a little dizzy. You take a deep gulp of water to help clear your mind. Suddenly, you hear a yell.

"We have a problem!" Sharif shouts. Erin is face down in the sand. She has heatstroke.

Tony sits down. "I can't go on anymore either," he says.

Turn the page.

"What should we do? Tony asks. "Is there any place we can find shelter?"

"We can't all stay here," Sharif says. "No one knows where we are except the people on the bus, and they're stuck."

It's clear to you that either you or Sharif need to continue on looking for help, and the other one needs to stay with Tony and Erin.

- To go for help, turn to page 28.
- To look for shelter, turn to page 31.

"I need to check out these animals," you say. The chance to see such amazing wildlife in its natural habitat is too awesome to pass up.

After another flight to Botswana, your group stands in front of a large Jeep. The driver from the Central Kalahari Game Reserve is friendly and eager to get you to your base camp.

"You are going to see some of the most majestic animals in the world," he says. "The Kalahari Basin is the world's largest continuous stretch of sand. It is a harsh environment for us, but the animals have adapted."

The desert stretches out for miles as you look out the window. You drive for several hours, daydreaming about wild animals. Suddenly, a loud *THUMP* jolts you out of your thoughts. The Jeep is stopped on the side of the road.

Turn the page.

"Apologies, but we have hit a rock," the driver says. "The car is damaged. You must walk the rest of the way to camp. It should only take a few hours."

Everyone looks defeated and a little worried. It's hot, and three hours walking in the desert could be dangerous. You're not even thinking of that, though.

"Seriously?" you mutter under your breath. "I came here to see animals not take the world's most miserable walk."

The driver hears and motions to you.

"If animals are what you want to see, I have a secret viewing area off the reserve path," he says. "If you stay and help me fix the truck, I will show you this area before going back to camp."

You are intrigued. Getting a chance to spot animals in the real wild could be dangerous. But it would also be special.

- To walk to the reserve, turn to page 26.
- To go with the driver, turn to page 37.

You decide to go to the reserve. It doesn't feel safe out here, and you don't want to be stuck in the African wilderness after dark.

The driver points the group in the direction of the reserve. You walk with Maria, who has her camera ready to take pictures. And while the driver said the trip to the reserve would be easy, no one is prepared for the heat and distance.

"This is miserable," Maria says.

So far, the only animals you've seen are a few stray birds and lizards.

Some safari adventure, you think.

After an hour of walking, everyone is hot and cranky. You're not sure you can take two more hours of this. It might make more sense to return to the Jeep and wait while the driver fixes it.

"Let's just go back to the Jeep," you say. "It's a thousand degrees, we're all tired, and the camp is nowhere in sight."

"We're already a third of the way there," a man named Ryan says. "And what if we go back, and the driver can't fix the Jeep?"

People begin murmuring. They seem to agree with Ryan.

"We're pressing forward," he says. "You can go back to the Jeep or come with us."

The group awaits your decision.

- To head back toward the Jeep, turn to page 39.
- To keep heading toward the reserve, turn to page 41.

"I'll keep going," you say. "Tony and Erin need your help. You know more about desert survival than I do."

"Okay, be careful," Sharif says.

You head out on your own, determined to find the village. You try to ration your water, but the heat is intense. It feels like you've been walking forever. You look down at your watch. It's been two hours.

I should have been there by now! you think to yourself.

You pull out the compass to make sure you're still going in the right direction. But when you look at it, the needle is zigzagging around. You shake your head and blink a few times to clear the fog. But the compass is still going crazy.

Just when you think all is lost, off in the distance you see a pool of water, surrounded by trees.

An oasis! you think. Picking up your pace, you head toward the beautiful sight. But you never get any closer to it. Meanwhile, the heat is searing. You close your eyes to gather yourself. But when you open them, the oasis is gone!

You spin around. Now it appears as if the oasis is on the other side of the desert. You stumble toward it. But it never gets any closer. You come to a horrible realization.

"It's not real," you mumble to yourself. Through your confusion, you realize you must have heat stroke. You're seeing things that aren't there. It's all a mirage.

Eventually, you fall to your knees. You're struggling just to keep your eyes open. You've always wanted to go to the Sahara Desert. But you didn't think you'd die there.

THE END

To follow another path, turn to page 9.
To learn more about survival in a desert, turn to page 101.

30

"I'll stay here with Tony and Erin," you say. "You keep going for help. You know the area better."

You watch Sharif walk off into the dunes as you try to wake Erin. Finally, she comes to.

"We need to get into the shade," you say.

Not too far away, you see a rocky outcropping. "There," you say. "Let's get some shade."

You and Tony help Erin to the cave-like structure. It is small, but it's enough for the group to crowd into and cool off. Your shirt is bright orange, so you rip off a bit of fabric and tie it to the rocks above the cave. Hopefully, it will help rescuers find you.

Turn the page.

You are amazed at this structure and how it has remained intact despite the harsh climate. As you examine the walls closely, you notice markings that appear to tell a story.

"Look!" you exclaim. "These are cave drawings! Ancient people used these to tell stories about how they hunted in this area."

Even though everyone is tired and hot, they gather around the drawings in excitement. It's a fascinating look into the past. For a minute, you've forgotten you are stranded in the Sahara.

The joy is short-lived, however. Tony kicks a rock in the cave, and a creature skitters out. It's a deathstalker scorpion! You try to push Tony out of the way, but it's too late. The scorpion stings him in the foot.

"OUCH!" Tony screams. He collapses to the ground in pain.

You watch as the scorpion leaves the cave. It isn't long before Tony can't move his leg. He has a terrible fever. Erin is still weak and dehydrated, and your water supply has run out.

With two injured people, nightfall approaching, and supplies dwindling, you're in a tight spot. You're losing hope when you hear something. It's Sharif!

"Thank goodness you put up that orange fabric," he says. "Or we wouldn't have found you."

Rescue workers have arrived. You're never been more relieved.

THE END

To follow another path, turn to page 9.
To learn more about survival in a desert, turn to page 101.

"I'll stay near the bus," you say. "Maybe I can do a little exploring while we wait."

As a group heads off to find help, you grab your bag and climb out of the bus. You have a small chisel and some brushes inside. These are the tools that fossil hunters use. You've read about fossils from dinosaurs and fish being found here.

"Don't go too far," Professor Tremblay shouts.

Amazingly, the Sahara Desert was once underwater. Over millions of years, however, the climate changed into the arid landscape for which it is now known.

You head toward an area that offers a little shade and begin gently chipping at the rock. It's unlikely you'll find anything, but it's a decent way to pass the time. It also helps you forget you're stuck in the desert.

Suddenly, your chisel makes a different sound. You look closely and begin to dig around the piece until you unearth it. You brush it off and hold it up to the daylight.

It looks like a tooth! you think.

You gather your belongings and sprint back to the bus just in time to hear the unmistakable sound of an engine starting.

"Look what I found!" you say to Professor Tremblay, who opens her eyes in shock when she sees your fossil.

Turn the page.

"Oh, my goodness, what a discovery," she says. "Archaeologists will want to explore here!"

"Now that the bus is working, we can catch up to the rest of the group and notify the authorities of what you've found," she adds.

You're thrilled as you climb back into the bus. You're holding ancient history in your hand! It was worth getting stranded. You can't wait to see what happens on the rest of the journey.

THE END

To follow another path, turn to page 9.
To learn more about survival in a desert, turn to page 101.

"I'm in!" you say to the driver, whose name turns out to be Agang. You and your friend Mike hang back to help him as the rest of the party heads to the reserve.

You spend some time repairing the truck. It's hot and dirty work. But after some time, Agang climbs into the seat. He cranks the engine, and after a few stutters, it roars to life. You and Mike cheer.

Agang climbs out and grabs his satchel. "Follow me," he says.

You head up the road a bit and then turn into a fenced area. There's a small gap in the fence. Agang pulls it back to allow you to squeeze through. There's a sign on the fence written in a foreign language.

"What does that say?" Mike asks.

"Danger," Agang responds. "Be very quiet in here. We don't want to scare anything."

The three of you slowly walk toward a clearing. As you reach it, you are stunned to see a host of wildebeests and kudu strolling through the desert. Giraffes crane their necks to reach food. You pull out your phone and snap photos.

Suddenly, all the animals look up and begin running. *What's going on?* you wonder.

Before you know it, there's a low growl behind you. You turn to see a black-maned lion! It's beautiful. But it's also deadly. And it's coming right for you! You have always wanted to see a lion, but it will be the last thing you ever see.

THE END

To follow another path, turn to page 9.
To learn more about survival in a desert, turn to page 101.

"I'm going back," you say. "Hopefully, the Jeep will be all fixed up. I'll see you at the reserve"

You hope someone will come along with you, but no one does. You head down the road into the dusty terrain. You didn't wear the best shoes for a long walk. Blisters are forming already.

You press on, in hopes the Jeep will come rumbling up the road at any moment. Your stomach growls with hunger. But there's nothing around except for a few springs of bushman grass.

A noise in the distance breaks the silence. It's a rhinoceros! Maybe there's some water nearby. You could really use a drink. You start heading toward the large animal, excited about the thought of getting close to the reserve and getting some water. But you move a little too fast given the blisters on your foot and turn your ankle.

Turn the page.

"Ow!" you yell, crumpling to the ground.

It's too painful to stand, let alone walk. You drag yourself along the dirt for a few feet before collapsing in exhaustion.

All you can do is yell for help. But with the sun beating down, you quickly tire. You close your eyes and wonder what to do next. After a few minutes, you hear voices!

You open your eyes to see some of the local Basarwa tribespeople. You point to your ankle. After some communicating through simple hand gestures, they pick you up and begin walking. You're safe for now, but you have no idea what these people plan to do with you. You hope you're able to somehow reunite with your group.

THE END

To follow another path, turn to page 9.
To learn more about survival in a desert, turn to page 101.

"Let's keep going," you say. You hope this is the right choice.

You walk slowly alongside Maria, who is clutching her camera.

"Maybe we'll see something cool," she says, hopefully. But you know she's as tired as you are.

The two of you slow your pace and let the rest of the group get ahead of you. Eventually, you lose sight of them altogether. Even though you are both tired, it's exciting to feel like you're on your own adventure together. Maria takes your picture with your arms spread out wide to show the large desert vista.

Suddenly, you see something that leaves you frozen in fear—a cheetah! The majestic animal is prowling in the distance, but close enough that it could reach you quickly given its speed.

Turn the page.

Maria takes a quick picture, and the cheetah's head snaps up.

"Let's move, quickly and quietly," you say.

You back away slowly until you find a bush to hide behind. You stay quiet for the next few minutes until the cheetah skulks away.

Then you hear the patter of footsteps and squeaks. A group of meerkats appear! They come close, curious about Maria's camera. One climbs on your foot! You're confused. Usually, these wild animals wouldn't be friendly with humans unless they were used to being around them.

As quickly as they appear, the meerkats scatter down the road. Just then, you hear some voices. It's a tour group from the reserve! They rush over to make sure you are safe. The rest of your group is with them.

"Welcome to the Kalahari," the leader says. "We were worried about your group. We decided to start searching for you. Thank goodness we found you before it got dark."

THE END

To follow another path, turn to page 9.
To learn more about survival in a desert, turn to page 101.

CHAPTER 3
HEADING TO ASIA

You have been fascinated with the continent of Asia for as long as you can remember. It is so large with such varying landscapes. Having already chosen to go to Asia, you have two options you can take. You can explore the hot Arabian Desert in Saudi Arabia, or you can help a respected scientist on her research in the icy Gobi Desert of Mongolia.

Turn the page.

You spent the time leading up to the trip reading about each desert and the characteristics and animals found in both. Either location would be incredible, but you've always been fascinated by scientific research.

You look over at your friend Will. You know he's leaning toward the Arabian Desert. It's where his ancestors are from. You must decide whether to go with your friend to see the desert of his dreams or to follow your own.

- To explore the Arabian Desert, go to page 47.
- To visit the Gobi Desert, turn to page 53.

"I want to go to the Arabian Desert," you say.

"Great!" Will says. "That's the one I choose as well."

You knew he would. You're excited to hang out with your friend and explore the desert.

When you land in Jeddah, Saudi Arabia, it's hard to imagine there's a huge desert anywhere near this bustling metropolis and its massive skyscrapers. But as you take the transport out to the camp, the desert slowly begins to take shape.

Before long, all traces of modern civilization have been swept away by sand dunes as far as the eye can see. There isn't even a road. Your driver follows the tracks of vehicles that came before him. He has to, or your vehicle will get stuck.

Turn the page.

The camp is set up with several canvas tents, so you will spend the night in the desert. The hot temperatures cool off at night. With a sky full of stars above, your eyes close quickly.

In the morning, you find Will standing at the activity sign-up sheet. You can either go on a camel excursion through the desert or soar above the sand in a hot air balloon.

"Let's go on the camels!" Will says.

You're more interested in the hot air balloon, but you did choose this location to have fun with your friend.

- To pick the camel ride, go to page 49.
- To choose the hot air balloon, turn to page 51.

"We can't come to the desert and not ride a camel," you say.

You walk over to a caravan of camels. They are almost seven feet tall! Unlike some of the other camels you've seen, the Arabian camel only has one hump. It is often called a dromedary.

The camels drink water in preparation for the desert trek, while the handlers prepare saddles for the riders. You pick out a quiet camel at the end of the row and softly pet its lowered head.

Turn the page.

"He likes you," the handler says. "He will take care of you."

You climb on using a step stool, and the camel begins to walk slowly. You feel like you've stepped into a history book.

"This is awesome!" Will yells.

After an hour riding, the group stops to let the animals to eat and drink. Will pulls you to the side.

"Let's do some exploring away from the group," he says. "We'll be back before the break is over."

You wouldn't mind getting away from the guides for a bit. They're very strict, and you feel like you're missing out on seeing some interesting areas. But you were thinking it might be best do to that while on the camels.

- To explore by foot, turn to page 57.
- To wait until you're back on your camels to explore, turn to page 59.

"I'm going to pick the hot air balloon," you say. "I've always wanted to go in one, and this might be my only chance."

Will is disappointed, but he understands. You agree to go your separate ways and tell each other all about your individual excursions later.

The group gathers in front of a huge, colorful balloon, and everyone loads in. Then the pilot goes through a complicated process of releasing bags tied to the balloon. He fires up a burner that shoots hot air into the balloon. It starts to rise!

The trip across the desert is breathtaking. The sunny day gives you a fantastic view of the dunes. The pilot points out unique animals like the oryx and the Arabian tahr grazing through the desert. You're especially excited to see the tahr, as they're endangered animals.

Turn the page.

The balloon lands so the group can have lunch and explore the area. You spot some animal footprints, and you're tempted to follow them. But is it safe to leave the group?

Arabian tahr

- To follow the footprints, turn to page 62.
- To stay with the group, turn to page 65.

"Helping a scientist with their research sounds cool," you say. "Plus, the cold never bothered me, anyway."

Will looks a bit disappointed, as he's decided to go to the Arabian Desert. But you both wish each other well and plan to catch up when you get back from your adventures.

You fly to Mongolia, eager to begin your scientific journey. You receive your first surprise as you trek from the airport to the research facility.

Unlike most deserts, the Gobi is not a sandy sprawl of land. It is mostly rocky and rough terrain, with the occasional sand dune. And there is definitely a chill in the air.

Few people wanted to come here. Your only group member here is Trina, who you don't know well. But you get to know each other on the ride. She is more friendly than you'd expected.

When you arrive at the research facility, a scientist comes out to greet you.

"My name is Dr. Hughes," she says. "Welcome to the Gobi," she says, spreading her arms. "It comes from a Mongolian word meaning 'very large and dry.' And that it is!"

You follow Dr. Hughes into the facility, which is filled with beakers, microscopes, and fossils. "Thank you for offering your assistance to our efforts," she says. "You can help track weather changes at our remote station or search for fossils near the mine."

- To track weather, go to page 55.
- To search for fossils, turn to page 70.

"I'll do the weather, if that's okay, Trina," you say. She nods her approval.

"Great!" Dr. Hughes says. "I'll give you all the tracking equipment, plus a walkie-talkie to stay in touch with us down here."

On the drive to the remote station, Dr. Hughes asks you a lot of questions about your interest in science. She also warns you that it will get extremely windy and cold overnight. Without any mountains to block it here, the wind plays a huge role in the freezing temperatures.

After you settle into the station, Dr. Hughes leaves. It's kind of creepy being alone here, but you busy yourself tracking the temperature and wind gauges and recording them on a chart. You feel like a real scientist!

Turn the page.

"How's it going up there?" your walkie-talkie squawks. It's Trina.

"Pretty good," you say. "Thanks for checking in. Over." The two of you chat back and forth until it's time to go to bed.

At bedtime, you wear several layers, as the temperature has dropped a lot. You fall asleep easily, but you are jolted awake by a howling wind. Suddenly, you realize the power and heat are off. The station is freezing. As you reach for the walkie-talkie, it falls to the ground and shatters.

You don't just want to sit and freeze. You recall that Dr. Hughes said there's a generator in a shed nearby. Or you can try to send a signal to the research facility using flares.

- To find the generator, turn to page 66.
- To try and shoot off a flare, turn to page 68.

While everyone else is eating, you and Will sneak away and head toward higher ground. You point out a few of the plants native to the Arabian Desert.

As you reach the top of the dune, you are excited to see some stones that appear to be ruins. You should probably get back to the group, but you're curious.

"Let's check out those stones," you say. Despite the heat, you move quickly.

As you get close to the stones, you take a funny step. Suddenly, you're sliding down and land with a *THUNK!* You stepped into a sinkhole! Pain shoots up your leg.

Will peers in from high above. You can only see a corner of his face because of the angle.

"Are you okay?" he yells.

Turn the page.

"No! I think I broke something," you say.

You look around. The sinkhole is too deep for you to climb out.

"I'll get help," Will says.

He disappears, leaving you alone. The minutes turn to hours. Did Will get lost on his way back? Did the sand blow your tracks away? Blowing sand is filling the sinkhole, slowly covering you, and the pain is becoming too much.

You hope Will finds the guides and returns soon. But the odds of finding you covered in a sinkhole are slim. You've never regretted anything more than you regret sneaking away from the guides.

THE END

To follow another path, turn to page 9.
To learn more about survival in a desert, turn to page 101.

"Let's wait until we get back on the camels," you say. "We can cover more ground that way."

Once the trek continues, you and Will look for an opportunity to break away. You get your chance when one of the other camels begins acting up. Your guide leaves to help calm the animal down. You and Will turn your camels sharply to the right and begin going down the side of a large dune, out of sight.

You feel guilty about leaving the guides, but you don't like feeling like they're babysitting you. It's only for a short time. Plus, you won't go far.

"You'll take care of me, right?" you say to your camel, patting its head.

As you continue to stroll, you notice some gazelles off in the distance.

Turn the page.

"Look!" you say to Will, pointing at them.

But you're not the only thing that sees the animals. A pair of wolves appear with an eye on the gazelles. When they notice you, they growl.

The camels are spooked. They both rise up. Will manages to hold on, but you're thrown off, hitting your head on the hard desert floor. The camels run away with surprising speed, taking Will with them. You're on your own.

Dazed, you see the wolves approaching. You stand up and raise your arms high in the air. You've learned that most predators run away if you make yourself look larger. Thankfully, that is just what the wolves do.

Your vision is blurry as you stumble along the desert. You have no idea which way you're going.

Just then, someone yells, "Stop!"

You snap into focus for a second. You're standing at the edge of a large precipice. One more step and you would have fallen into a sinkhole.

You turn around to see your guide. You're safe for now, but the concussion you've suffered means you must end your trip and go home. You're disappointed, but you know it's your own fault.

THE END

To follow another path, turn to page 9.
To learn more about survival in a desert, turn to page 101.

You want to see if these prints belong to a tahr. Just imagine seeing an endangered animal up close! You follow the footprints for a while. Just as you decide you should probably get back, you see the balloon rising into the air. The pilot must have miscounted the number of passengers! Worse yet, you're in the shade of a dune, so it's difficult for the rest of the group to spot you.

"Wait!" you shout, waving your arms. But the balloon is too high for anyone to see or hear you.

You think you can make your way back following the flight path of the balloon, but it's going much faster than you expected. Now, there's nothing around but sand. You start the slow walk back to camp, using your compass.

But your canteen is low, and you don't have any food. If you don't find the camp soon, you may not make it. As you come around a bend, you see a beautiful horse standing in front you. You think it might be a mirage, but the horse approaches you.

"Are you lost?" you ask your new friend. "Me too."

Turn the page.

As you take the horse's reins, it begins walking with a purpose. It seems to know where it is going, so you follow. Before long, you see some makeshift tents and structures. It's a Bedouin camp!

The people rejoice as you lead the horse into camp. You have returned something very important. People bow and grasp your hand.

"I am lost," you say.

A man comes forward. He understands your attempts at explaining where your camp is.

The group will take you back. You are returning as a hero!

THE END

To follow another path, turn to page 9.
To learn more about survival in a desert, turn to page 101.

Staying with the group is the smart thing to do. You have a nice lunch with the folks in your group and walk together exploring the various dunes, plants, and rock formations. Finally, it is time to return to camp. That evening, you and Will meet up to discuss your adventures.

"The camels were really cool," Will says. "But the guides were super strict. I wanted to wander off on my own, but I was too afraid to do it alone."

"The balloon was fun too," you say. "The view from above the desert is just incredible."

You were afraid Will would be upset that you didn't go with him, but he's not. You both had a great day, and you can't wait to see what tomorrow brings.

THE END

To follow another path, turn to page 9.
To learn more about survival in a desert, turn to page 101.

You have to try to get the generator started. As you open the door to the facility, you're hit with a blast of freezing wind. You've never been this cold in your life. But the shed is close. You'll just run there and back. It will be quicker than putting on all of your winter gear.

You close the door behind you and walk toward the shed. The wind is making it nearly impossible to see, blowing sand and pebbles into your face. You reach the shed and stumble along until you find the generator.

You open the control panel on the machine and flip the switch to start it. Nothing happens. You find a crank on the back of the machine and wind it several times. The machine remains silent. After closer examination with your flashlight, you see green fluid on the ground.

A leak! you realize with dismay. It's the coolant that helps keep the generator running.

"Okay, back to the lab," you say aloud. But your words slur. And your hands are starting to tingle. Uh oh. You're probably getting hypothermia.

Just then, your flashlight goes out. You try to run toward the lab, but you stumble. Your legs are too stiff to move. You're getting more confused. Frostbite is setting in. You fall to the ground and hope someone finds you before you freeze to death.

THE END

To follow another path, turn to page 9.
To learn more about survival in a desert, turn to page 101.

You decide to signal the research lab. You can see the lights of the lab in the distance, so you hope they'll be able to see your signal. You rummage through the supply cabinet and find a couple of flares. But you need to figure out the best place to put them so Dr. Hughes can see that you need help.

You peek out the window and see a slight rise in elevation in the distance.

"That will work," you say to yourself. You put on your heavy coat, gloves, and boots and step outside. The cold stings your face.

Walking uphill is difficult. The wind blows straight at you. When you reach the top, you pull out the flare. You open the top, strike it, and it won't light. It must have gotten wet at some point. You only have one flare left. You hope it lights.

You take a deep breath and strike it. It works! As it brightens the area, you see a pair of eyes in the distance. A creature slowly emerges. It's a snow leopard! The animal eyes you warily. You stay completely still. After a few minutes, it trots away.

Soon, you hear an engine. You see the headlights of a car. You run toward the building. It's Trina and Dr. Hughes!

"We were worried about you when we couldn't get you on the walkie-talkie," Trina says.

"I saw a snow leopard!" you tell the doctor.

"We've always wondered if we had one out here!" she says. "Having proof will help my research. Their habits and the weather patterns are often linked. Now let's get you warm."

THE END

To follow another path, turn to page 9.
To learn more about survival in a desert, turn to page 101.

"I'd like to search for fossils," you say.

The next morning, you wake up excited about the chance to explore the fossil-rich area. Dr. Hughes tells you about sand slides. These were avalanches of waterlogged sand that flowed down sand dunes thousands of years ago, trapping ancient creatures.

"The sand slides kept the remains of unsuspecting animals preserved," Dr. Hughes tells you. "Scientists have discovered dinosaur eggs in the region. If you found one, you'd be famous!"

Dr. Hughes gives you a tool kit and takes you to an abandoned mine, where a dig site has already been set up. You're not working on the main excavation, but a smaller site that has been set up for you to help prepare for a later dig.

She shows you how to slowly remove layers of dirt before heading back to the lab. The work is slow and tedious, but you're still hoping to aid in finding something special.

The sound of your tools picking at the dirt is interrupted by a noise coming from the mine. You edge closer to the opening, and the sound grows louder. You don't want an animal to mess up the excavation site. You grab your flashlight and use the rope to lower yourself into the mine.

Turn the page.

As you climb down makeshift stairs, the mine gets darker, and the air gets stuffy. But the noise grows louder. You flash your light into a corner and see a goat! As you move toward the animal, you notice there are some babies nearby as well.

Goats are everywhere in the Gobi. This one must have fallen into the mine and given birth!

"I'll get you some help," you say to the poor creatures. You pull on the rope to climb back out, but it snaps off! You can't reach the ledge to get back out of the mine. You're stuck!

You go back to the goats and offer the mother and her babies some fruit from your pack. They eat hungrily. You sit down and wonder what to do next. Some of the baby goats nuzzle against your body for warmth.

After a while, you can tell the sun is setting. You know Dr. Hughes is coming back for you soon. You use your flashlight to signal out of the hole. Every so often, you call out for help. Finally, you hear a voice! It's Dr. Hughes calling for you.

"Down here!" you yell.

"Oh, no!" she says. "I'll get you out!"

The goats crowd around you. You may not have found a fossil, but you did help save some beautiful creatures.

THE END

To follow another path, turn to page 9.
To learn more about survival in a desert, turn to page 101.

CHAPTER 4
QUEST DOWN UNDER

While all the choices sound interesting, only one takes you to the land down under. The trip takes place during the Australia winter, so the temperatures won't be as hot as in the summer.

"I'm going to Australia," you say. "I've always wanted to see a kangaroo."

I chose Australia too," your friend Marcus says. "I have family that lives near the desert, so hopefully I can visit them."

Turn the page.

You spend most of the plane ride to Perth reading about the kangaroos of the Australian outback. As the plane descends, a sheet is passed between your group to determine your final destination.

When you land, the group will break up into two excursions. One will explore the vast Great Victoria Desert with its huge sand dunes. Another will head to the isolated Great Sandy Desert, home to the landmark Ayers Rock.

"Hey," Marcus says from across the aisle. "What excursion are you going to do?"

- To travel to the Great Victoria Desert, go to page 77.
- To trek to the Great Sandy Desert, turn to page 83.

"I'm going to the Great Victoria," you say.

"Me too!" Marcus says.

The two of you gather your bags at the airport and pile into the bus going to the nature lodge. As the city gives way to the desert, you start to notice holes in the ground near some of the dunes. You remember reading about how the indigenous people of Australia create water wells to help them survive the harsh desert conditions.

By the time you arrive at the lodge, darkness is approaching. You hear sounds from animals that you've never heard before.

You listen as the nature guide explains the options for activities tomorrow, including an all-terrain vehicle ride in the desert. It sounds like fun!

Turn the page.

"My relatives live near here," Marcus says. "I arranged to spend tomorrow with them. Do you want to come along? They'll know the local sights."

You like the idea of learning from the locals. On the other hand, riding an ATV through the desert is a once-in-a-lifetime experience.

- To do the ATV trip, go to page 79.
- To visit Marcus's family, turn to page 81.

"Thanks for the offer," you say to Marcus. "But I think I'm going to stay here and ride ATVs."

"No problem," he says. "Let me know how it goes!"

The next morning, you are partnered with a guide named Tom. You slide behind him on the vehicle.

"We're off," he says, revving the engine.

The ride through the desert is exhilarating. You see the sun rise over the dunes, and lizards scatter out of your path. It's a beautiful ride, but a little slow for you.

"Can we go a little faster?" you ask Tom.

"I'm not supposed to, but you asked for it, mate," Tom says, speeding up.

Turn the page.

You're thrilled as the ATV bounds over the desert hills. Suddenly, the vehicle slides on the loose pebbles of the desert floor. You go flying off and bang your head. Even though you're wearing a helmet, everything goes black.

When you wake up, you hear moaning in the distance. You stumble to the overturned ATV. Tom is trapped!

"My leg," he says. "It's stuck."

"I'll get some help," you say. You look around. You're not sure where you are. To the northeast is a big dune, and to the southwest is a small rocky outcropping. Getting to higher ground may help you get a better idea of your surroundings. The dune is higher, but the path toward the rocks is on the way back to camp.

- To climb the dune, turn to page 87.
- To head toward the rocks, turn to page 90.

"Are you sure your family wouldn't mind?" you ask.

"Not at all!" Marcus says. "My great-uncle will pick us up in the morning. He is from the Anangu tribe. They are the native people of this area."

You and Marcus are waiting at the gates of the lodge the next morning when a small motorcycle and sidecar pulls up. An older man gets off and hugs Marcus.

"Hello," he says to you. "I am Marcus's uncle Daku."

You ride in the sidecar to the village, where Marcus is greeted warmly by his relatives. After lunch, Daku points to a rocky outcropping in the distance.

Turn the page.

"You two should explore our local rock art," he says. "Our ancestors created these paintings using beeswax and clay. They are sacred."

You and Marcus walk about a mile to see this ancient art. It is amazing to see these images preserved after thousands of years.

"Maybe we should head back now," you say. "Your uncle can drive us back to camp."

"Sure," Marcus says reaching for a loose rock. "I just want to grab a rock to take as a souvenir."

You don't think Marcus should take the rock. This is ancient history, and it probably should be left alone. But it IS just a rock. Is it worth saying something?

- To stop Marcus from taking the rock, turn to page 92.
- To not say anything, turn to page 94.

The pen hovers over the paper before you make a final decision.

"I'm going to the Great Sandy Desert," you tell Marcus. "There are a couple of landmarks I really want to visit there."

You pull out your notebook and study your research on ergs. These seas of sand are formed in parallel shapes from winds blowing the same direction for a long time.

The Great Sandy has amazing ergs. Its dunes run more than 25 miles in the same direction.

Upon landing, your group heads to the small camp on the edge of the desert. It will serve as your jumping-off point. There you meet a group of adventurers from Amsterdam, who are all very friendly.

Turn the page.

Tomorrow morning, you plan to take a helicopter ride over the desert. You find yourself chatting with a girl named Emma about it. Before you know it, everyone is preparing for bed.

"After everyone's asleep, let's sneak out and do some stargazing," Emma suggests. "This is one of the best places in the world to see the night sky."

You would like to check out the stars, but you don't want to risk oversleeping and missing the helicopter tour.

- To go to bed, go to page 85.
- To go stargazing first, turn to page 99.

"I'm going to sleep," you say. "I don't want to be tired for the tour tomorrow." You gather your belongings and head to bed.

The next morning, you wake refreshed and ready for the helicopter tour. Because the groups are so big, the tours will have to go in stages. You are in the second group. When the first tour returns, you see Emma walk by with a big smile on her face.

"It's amazing," she says. "Enjoy it."

You climb aboard the small helicopter and try to forget your nerves. It rises up over the desert landscape. The dunes come into view. They look like plowed fields because they are so long and straight.

SQUEE! SQUEE! A loud alarm starts going off inside the cockpit.

"Hold on, everyone!" the pilot shouts.

The helicopter starts twirling out of control. You brace for impact as the helicopter slams into the sand.

After recovering from the jolt, you unbuckle yourself. The other passengers are either unconscious . . . or worse.

You are able to wriggle out of the damaged door. The pilot isn't moving. The radio is crushed. Should you go searching for help or stay with the helicopter?

- To search for help, turn to page 95.
- To stay with the helicopter, turn to page 97.

You head toward the dune in hopes that higher ground will provide you with a better vantage point. The dune is covered with small shrubs that you grab as you climb.

When you reach the top, you are surprised to hear the rumble of thunder. The skies quickly open, and it begins pouring rain. You never would have expected a storm to hit in the desert, but it does happen occasionally.

Turn the page.

Through the rain, it's nearly impossible to figure out which way to go for help. You shield your eyes with your hand and walk toward a gnarled tree. The rain begins to ease as you approach. Just then, you stumble on what appears to be a flat rock.

"YOUCH!" you exclaim, as pain radiates from your toe.

There's a flash of movement and a poke on your leg. You look down and see a long brown snake flashing its fangs. You've been bitten!

This part of the Australian desert has some of the deadliest snakes in the world. You groan in agony as your leg starts swelling. It won't take long for the snake's venom to make its way through your body.

You stumble forward. Your whole body goes numb! All you can do now is slide across the desert floor. The poison is too much to overcome. The desert has claimed another victim. If only you hadn't asked Tom to speed up. Your last thought is that you hope someone comes along to help him.

THE END

To follow another path, turn to page 9.
To learn more about survival in a desert, turn to page 101.

You head toward the rocks hoping to see the lodge in this direction. As you do, the sky opens up into a downpour! Just then, you remember that the Great Victoria does get occasional storms.

You can hardly see through the rain, but you have to carry on. Tom needs help. After what feels like an hour, you still see no signs of civilization. As you debate whether to turn back, you see movement in the brush. It's a baby red kangaroo!

The joey might be in distress. You look around for the mother, knowing that it will protect its young. You don't see her, so you approach the joey carefully. You don't want to touch it. Human contact could cause the young creature to be left out of the mob.

The joey appears to be healthy, so you'll leave it alone. If you weren't lost, you'd be thrilled to be this close to a kangaroo!

Then you hear footsteps approaching behind you. You turn to see an angry adult kangaroo headed your way. You back away quickly but not fast enough. The 'roo jumps and kicks at you. While you turn to avoid the full blast, the kick nails you in the arm, knocking you to the ground.

You run away grasping your arm. You think it might be broken. As you scramble over a small dune, you see several people on ATVs.

"Help!" you scream.

When they see you they rush to your side. You explain about the ATV crash and your arm. You're whisked away to the lodge. You hope that Tom is okay and that the search party finds him quickly.

THE END

To follow another path, turn to page 9.
To learn more about survival in a desert, turn to page 101.

"I don't think you should take that," you tell Marcus. "Didn't your uncle say this place was sacred?"

"Oh, you're right!" Marcus says. "I'll just take some photos instead."

You and Marcus pose in front of the rock art and take some incredible photos. Your friends and family back home will love these.

Then you walk back to the village and enjoy a lovely dinner before Marcus's uncle drives you back to your camp.

"Thank you so much, Uncle Daku," Marcus says.

"It was my pleasure, nephew," he says. "I hope you will come and visit us again sometime—both of you."

You are honored to have been included. You had come to see the Great Victorian Desert, but you never expected to make friends with the native people of the area. What an incredible experience!

THE END

To follow another path, turn to page 9.
To learn more about survival in a desert, turn to page 101.

You don't want to tell Marcus what to do. As he grabs the rock, a redback spider crawls out and bites his hand! Marcus starts sweating. His arm is swelling.

"I'll go for help," you tell him. "Stay here!"

You run back to Uncle Daku's village and tell him what happened. You both hop on his motorcycle and rush to Marcus. When you find him, he is in pain and feverish.

"We'll need to get you to the closest clinic," Daku says. "They'll have antivenom there."

It's hours to the closest clinic, but Marcus makes it in time. You're relieved he's going to be okay. But you wish you'd have told him not to touch that rock.

THE END

To follow another path, turn to page 9.
To learn more about survival in a desert, turn to page 101.

People are hurt. You need to find help sooner rather than later. Before heading off, you write HELP in the sand, but the wind soon erases your letters.

You decide to walk back to the lodge. The heat saps your energy. You're moving slow. But when you see what looks like a road in the distance, you get a burst of energy. If you can get there, maybe you can flag someone down.

Suddenly, you hear a loud noise nearby. You turn to see a wild camel charging at you, frothing at the mouth. You dive out of the way just in time, and the animal storms off into the distance. Your heart pounds in relief. You'd been so obsessed with kangaroos that you forgot about Australia's wild camels. They can be aggressive to people, especially if they've recently given birth.

Turn the page.

You reach the road just in time to see a pair of headlights in the distance. You stand in the middle of the road, waving your arms frantically. It's a bus from the camp!

You tell them about the crash. They radio to the authorities. They ask you about the location of the crash site, but you're not sure how to direct them there.

An emergency helicopter search begins of the entire area. You can only hope that they find the crash site in time to help everyone. You can't help but wonder if it would have been smarter of you to stay at the crash site.

THE END

To follow another path, turn to page 9.
To learn more about survival in a desert, turn to page 101.

Staying with the helicopter seems like the safest bet. That way you can tend to the injured and signal anyone who may come along.

You find a flare in what remains of the helicopter and scramble to the top of the dune. It seems to stretch endlessly in both directions. Next, you light the flare and stick it in the sand. You wait for 20 minutes, but no one comes.

You decide to start a fire to draw attention. You gather some of the spinifex grass found nearby and place it inside of a collection of rocks. You also add some paper from your notebook.

You take a signal flare and light it. You touch it to the grass and paper and watch a flame slowly grow. Once the fire is burning, you take a blanket from your pack. You cover two of the injured people. You have to get them help soon.

Turn the page.

You remember learning Morse code so you signal S-O-S in the smoke to anyone who sees it. You hope it works as you watch the fire go out.

After making sure everyone is still breathing inside the copter, you sit down to rest. You must have closed your eyes because you are awakened to someone shouting.

You scramble to your feet. "We need help!" you say. The man slides down the dune, speaking into a radio. "I saw your signal," he says. "Great job. Help is on the way."

Before long, you hear the blades of another helicopter heading toward you. As much as you'd like to avoid ever traveling that way again, you're happy that you've been rescued.

THE END

To follow another path, turn to page 9.
To learn more about survival in a desert, turn to page 101.

"Let's meet up in an hour," you say.

Together, you lie on a large sand dune in the moonlight. The dazzlingly starlit sky is amazing. Suddenly, you feel a prick on your foot. You shine your flashlight on several desert scorpions.

"I think I just got stung!" you shout.

"Ouch! Me too!" Emma says.

Your feet are swelling. The two of you hobble back to camp, screaming in pain. The nurse rushes out. She gives you both pain reliever and ice packs.

"The effects will wear off in a few hours," she says. "But you'll need to stay in bed tomorrow."

No helicopter ride for you. You only have yourself to blame for missing out.

THE END

To follow another path, turn to page 9.
To learn more about survival in a desert, turn to page 101.

CHAPTER 5
BE PREPARED

No one wants to be stranded in the desert. The harsh conditions, brutal weather, and limited population make survival difficult for even the most experienced adventurer. But there are steps you can take to help you survive in any environment if you are lost.

The wilderness rule of threes says a person can survive three minutes without air, three hours without shelter, three days without water, and three weeks without food, but that doesn't fully account for the extreme nature of deserts.

The most important element of desert survival is planning and preparation. Know how you're going to get in and out of a desert environment. Know where you'll be staying and how you'll keep yourself hydrated. And always let people know where you'll be. That way, if they don't hear from you, they'll have an idea of where to look.

Many desert experts only travel at night. That way, the hot sun doesn't sap their energy, and it will allow their body to retain more water. During the day, stay in the shade when you can.

If you are in some sort of accident, don't abandon your vehicle. While it seems like leaving to find help would be beneficial, the car, ATV, helicopter, or whatever vehicle has broken down is more useful to you. Open the doors, pop the hood, honk the horn, and use the mirrors to reflect light. These are all signals that pilots and other rescue workers look for to help find people who have gotten lost.

Of course, you should have plenty of water and food on hand. Eating food can make you thirsty, so try to conserve your food supply as much as possible.

If you find yourself out of water, follow these tips to try to locate a source:

- Look for vegetation.
- Search rocky areas to see if water has collected there after a storm.
- Gather dew from rocks or plants.
- Look for animal tracks and follow them. Animals will know where local water sources are.

Finally, try to stay calm. Getting lost in the desert would be a stressful situation for anyone, but often, poor decisions are made when panic has clouded your judgement. Keep your wits about you, stay safe, and conserve your energy.

TRUE STORIES OF SURVIVAL

JAMES RILEY AND CREW

JAMES RILEY

In 1815, American captain James Riley and his crew were caught in a damaged ship limping across the coast of North Africa. They were captured and sold into enslavement. They were forced to go on a journey through the Sahara Desert filled with death, dehydration, and ill treatment from hostile tribes. They roamed the desert for more than a month until a weakened Riley convinced his captors that he was a prominent official and would be worth a hearty reward. While that was not true, a British government official did eventually pay his ransom, setting Riley and his crew free.

MAURO PROSPERI

In 1994, Italian policeman Mauro Prosperi entered an extreme long-distance race called Marathon des Sables in Morocco. It was a six-day race through the Sahara Desert. While racing, a sandstorm blew in. The storm knocked Prosperi off course and confused his sense of direction. He was forced to lick dew off rocks and suck on wet wipes for moisture. He wandered the desert for nine days and 180 miles before he stumbled across a village. He lost 35 pounds during his ordeal. But he returned to the race in 2012 and completed it.

ROBERT BOGUCKI

In 1999, Alaskan volunteer firefighter Robert Bogucki traveled to the Great Sandy Desert to bike and hike across the Outback. After a couple weeks, tourists found his abandoned bike. After another 12 days of searching, authorities called off the operation. But his parents refused to believe their son had died, so they hired their own search party. He was eventually found by a news team in a helicopter 43 days after he had gone missing, in relatively good shape. He survived by finding water holes and eating vegetation he discovered in the desert.

ROBERT BOGUCKI

S.T.O.P. TO SURVIVE

The best way to remember what to do if you find yourself in an emergency situation is to S.T.O.P. Each letter stands for an instruction you can follow to help get yourself to safety.

S.T.O.P.: Stop, Think, Observe, Plan

Stop: Stay calm and take in the situation.

Think: What do you need to do to survive? What supplies do you have on hand that you could use?

Observe: Look around. Do you see familiar landmarks? Can you tell what direction you're pointed?

Plan: Make a plan of action and never give up.

OTHER PATHS TO EXPLORE

1. Many extreme desert environments are home to either wandering tribes or Indigenous peoples. How do you think they survive in those extreme conditions? How might they find food and water? What would it be like to have little technology or contact with the outside world? How do they survive surrounded by dangerous wildlife?

2. Imagine you are a parent, and your child wants to explore a potentially dangerous desert as part of a school group or class project. How do you support your child's interest, while also keeping them safe? Would you let them take part? Why or why not?

3. You are a rescue worker in Australia. You've treated hundreds of people who have hurt themselves in major or minor ways by not making the proper preparations before heading into the desert. You're considering starting a blog to warn tourists of the dangers that can occur if people don't take the desert seriously. What are some of the topics you should write about? What advice would you give your readers?

GLOSSARY

chisel (CHIZ-uhl)—a tool with a flat, sharp end used to cut stone or wood

concussion (kuhn-KUH-shuhn)—an injury to the brain caused by a hard blow to or sudden motion of the head

dehydration (dee-hy-DRAY-shuhn)—a life-threatening medical condition caused by a lack of water

mirage (muh-RAZH)—something that appears to be there but is not; mirages are caused by light rays bending where air layers of different temperatures meet

murmur (MUHR-muhr)—a quiet, blurred sound

oasis (oh-AY-siss)—a place in a desert where there is water for plants, animals, and people

plume (PLOOM)—a long cloud of smoke or vapor resembling a feather

ration (RASH-uhn)—a fixed portion of food or other goods

vast (VAST)—very great in size, amount or intensity

READ MORE

Crane, Cody. *Deserts in Danger.* New York: an imprint of Scholastic, Inc. 2024

Jaycox, Jaclyn. *This or That Questions About the Desert.* North Mankato, MN: Capstone, 2022.

Munro, Roxie. *A Day in the Life of a Desert: 6 Desert Habitats, 108 Species, and How to Save Them.* New York: Holiday House, 2023.

INTERNET SITES

Britannica: Desert
britannica.com/science/desert

Sandstorms in the Sahara Desert: Top Causes and Frequency
a-z-animals.com/blog/sandstorms-in-the-sahara-desert/

World Heritage Convention: Central Kalahari Game Reserve
whc.unesco.org/en/tentativelists/5555/

ABOUT THE AUTHOR

Elliott Smith is a freelance writer, editor, and author. He has covered a wide variety of subjects, including sports, entertainment, and travel, for newspapers, magazines, and web sites. He has written more than 70 children's books, both fiction and nonfiction. He lives in the Washington, D.C., area with his wife and two children.